STUDENTS BEWARE:
LIFE DOES NOT BEGIN AT 21

A Federal Government
Pre-employment
Background Investigation Guidebook

By Investigator

LORRAINE KOSTER

iUniverse, Inc.
New York   Bloomington

Students Beware: Life Does Not Begin at 21
A Federal Government Pre-Employment Background Investigation Guidebook

iUniverse books may be ordered through booksellers or by contacting:

iUniverse
1663 Liberty Drive
Bloomington, IN 47403
www.iuniverse.com
1-800-Authors (1-800-288-4677)

ISBN: 978-0-595-47703-6 (pbk)
ISBN: 978-0-595-50442-8 (cloth)
ISBN: 978-0-595-91966-6 (ebk)

Printed in the United States of America

A NOTE FROM THE AUTHOR

This is a work of nonfiction. Please note that the information contained in this book was accurate at the time of writing. It is important to remember that federal laws, regulations, policies, and procedures are subject to change. Any questions about the contents should be directed to the federal agency involved in your endeavor.

To my grandchildren:
Christopher, Breanan, and Cameron Silzer;
Lauren and Madison Gonzalez.
And to
Jack Withers for his patience and support.

Contents

PART FOUR
Investigators at Work

Introduction

Many young people believe that accountability doesn't begin until the age of twenty-one. The reality is, it begins well before then. What you do in your high school and college years may significantly impact your future. Often, choices made during these years can help or hinder your future career opportunities.

Students Beware: Life Does Not Begin at 21 is a guidebook to help you understand the process that takes place during pre-employment background investigations for positions within the federal government. Some of the information is of a general nature, as agencies sometimes have their own special needs and requests. The objective here is to provide a basic understanding of federal employment policies and procedures.

Part 1 of this book contains information applicable to most federal government pre-employment background investigations. Part 2 contains general information about federal career opportunities and the federal application process. Part 3 details the federal employment investigation process. Finally, Part 4 explains what investigators scrutinize during the field investigation.

It is my hope that this book will show you the importance of acting responsibly during your earlier years. I have over twenty years of investigative experience working with government and the private sector. Sadly, I have seen people lose desired opportunities because of poor choices they have made. If I can help just a few people make it easier for themselves to achieve their desired goals, my effort in writing this book will have been worthwhile.

PART ONE

General Information

Chapter 1
A Look at Federal Employment
Investigation History

Federal pre-employment background investigations procedures have evolved over the years, becoming more organized and uniform. The following is a brief history of how the process has evolved.

Civil Service Commission (CSC)

In 1883, Congress passed the Civil Service Commission Act. The CSC Act empowered the president to establish rules to determine the fitness of persons applying for public service positions. It authorized the CSC to conduct investigations to enforce civil service laws, as well as federal rules and regulations. Early investigations focused primarily on misconduct or fraud found in the examination process. At that time, the CSC had no permanent investigative units. Staff evaluated the fitness of applicants by reviewing information contained in employment questionnaires.

A major change occurred during World War I because there was a need for a large number of qualified and loyal government employees. In 1917, President Woodrow Wilson issued Executive Order 2569 (an executive order is a directive from the president that is binding upon the executive branch of government). This executive order required the CSC to investigate the qualifications, fitness, and character of applicants applying for some postmaster positions. This was so effective that in the 1920s, the CSC established the Division of Investigations and Review. The CSC expanded to conduct background investigations for federal law enforcement positions.

National security concerns called for more changes. In 1953, President Dwight Eisenhower issued Executive Order 10450, establishing a program to conduct national security and suitability background investigations of present and future federal employees. This executive order stated that in the interest of national security, federal employees must be reliable, trustworthy, of good conduct and character, and be loyal to the United States government. The CSC was the appointed authority to implement the order.

Further changes were made in 1954, when President Eisenhower signed Executive Order 10577; this gave the CSC authority to adopt rules and regulations to have oversight into the examination and investigative process for federal employment. Also in 1954, the Atomic Energy Act was established, giving the CSC federal authority to conduct background investigations for the Department of Energy (DOE), formerly the Atomic Energy Commission.

Over twenty years passed until the government implemented other major changes. In 1978, under President Jimmy Carter, the Civil Service Reform Act dictated the suitability of investigations. This act replaced the older Civil Service rules. In 1979, the CSC reorganized to become the United States Office of Personnel Management (OPM). OPM assumed the responsibility of conducting federal employment background investigations unless a federal agency head chooses to implement the executive order.

Further changes came in 1991, when President George H. Bush signed National Security Directive 63: Single Scope Background Investigations. This directive set minimum investigative standards for executive departments and agencies granting individuals access to Top Secret (TS) national security information and Sensitive Compartmented Information (SCI).

United States Office of Personnel Management (OPM)

OPM headquarters is located in Washington, D.C., with branch offices in various parts of the country. OPM continues to conduct employment background investigations for most federal agencies and their contractors. Some of the better-known defense contractors include: The Boeing Co., Inc., General Dynamics Corporation, Litton Industries, Inc., The Lockheed Martin Corporation, Northrop-Grumman Corporation, Rockwell International Corporation, and TRW, Incorporated. OPM has a federal workforce of approximately two thousand that includes investigators and support staff. In addition, their contractor staff also includes about six thousand field investigators and support personnel. Further information can be found at www.opm.gov.

Privatization

In 1996, Congress passed an initiative allowing privatization of some investigative portions of OPM. Thus, the employee-owned stock ownership company, United States Investigations Services, Inc. (USIS) was formed. Today, USIS is the largest supplier of background investigations for the federal government. Their main government affiliate is OPM. They have a support staff of over three thousand, including field investigators nationwide. Under contract with OPM, they perform background investigations for many federal departments and agencies, including the

Department of Defense, Department of Homeland Security, Department of State, and the National Intelligence Community Department—to name a few. USIS also conducts private industry investigations on a contract basis.

In 2003, Walsh, Carson, Anderson & Stowe, a private firm specializing in information services, communications, and health care, purchased USIS. The company continues to contract for the same government services. Further information is on their Web site at www.usis.com.

Other private investigation firms have signed contracts to conduct background and security investigations for OPM. Most contracted investigation firms operate as agents for OPM.

Defense Security Services (DSS)

Another major player in protecting national security is DSS, a Department of Defense (DOD) agency. DSS was formerly Defense Investigation Service (DIS). DSS was founded in 1972 to consolidate DOD Personnel Security Investigations. Prior to that, four DOD agencies (the U.S. Army Intelligence Command, the U.S. Army Criminal Investigations Command, the Naval Investigative Service, and the Air Force Office of Special Investigations) did these security investigations. In February 2005, DOD contracted with OPM to handle some of their background investigations.

Today, DSS continues to play a major role in protecting national security interests. In addition, as stated on their Web site, "The Defense Security Services (DSS) administers the National Industrial Security Program (NISP) on behalf of the Department of Defense as well as 23 non-DOD federal agencies with the Executive Branch. Presently, DSS has Industrial Security oversight for over 12,000 cleared facilities participating in the NISP." DSS also maintains a DSS Academy that provides security education and training to DOD and other U.S. government personnel, employees of U.S. government contractors, and authorized employees of foreign governments. DSS also administers the Arms, Ammunition and Explosives (AA&E) program, and the Critical Infrastructure Program (CIP). Both provide protection for the critical assets of DOD.

Federal Bureau of Investigation (FBI)

The FBI was born in 1908 during the presidency of Theodore Roosevelt. Its mission is: "To protect and defend the United States against terrorist and foreign intelligence threats, to uphold and enforce the criminal laws of the United States, and to provide leadership and criminal justice services to federal, state, municipal, and international agencies and partners." In addition, the agency manages background investigations on persons who apply for positions with the FBI and other government entities such as the White House, Department of Justice, Administrative Office of the U.S. Courts, and certain House and Senate committees. Additional information about the FBI can be found at www.fbi.gov.

Note that agency authority for federal background investigations is subject to change.

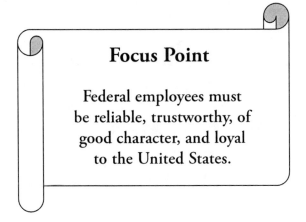

Focus Point

Federal employees must
be reliable, trustworthy, of
good character, and loyal
to the United States.

Chapter 2
Federal Career Opportunities

The federal government is the largest employer in the United States. According to federal employment statistics in the year 2000, there were 1,784,032 employees in the executive branch of government. This does not include the United States Postal Service (USPS) that has over 700,000 career employees. There are countless career opportunities. Most positions offer medical plans, pension plans, and retirement benefits. There is also the opportunity for advancement within an agency, or transfer to other federal agencies. Job security is also an advantage to federal employment, although it is not guaranteed.

The largest human resource agency for the federal government is the United States Office of Personnel Management (OPM). As you have previously learned, they are responsible for assisting many federal agencies with the hiring process and/or employment background investigations. The following are some examples:

Federal Agencies That Receive Assistance From OPM

Department of Agriculture
Army Corps of Engineers
Bureau of Customs & Border Patrol
Bureau of Land Management
Defense Security Services
Department of Commerce
Department of Defense
Department of Health & Human Services
Department of Homeland Security
Defense Intelligence Agency
Department of Interior
Department of Justice
Department of Labor
Federal Trade Commission
General Services Agency
National Archives & Records
National Security Agency
Nuclear Regulatory Commission
Peace Corps
Social Security Administration
Department of State
Department of Transportation
Department of Treasury
Department of Veterans Affairs
United States Attorneys Office

To search job openings, go to the Web site of United States Office of Personnel Management at www.opm.gov. Click on "Career Opportunities," then "USA Jobs," and next "Search Jobs." You can find job openings by entering job titles or a location (city, state, or zip code). Under each job opening, there is a listing of opening dates, job summary, agency, and location. This Web site is extensive. You can explore over 70,000 federal jobs. If you click on "My USA Jobs," you can become a member and post your resume online to allow recruiters to contact you. You can also apply for federal government jobs and receive automated job alerts. To become a member, you need to enter a username and password.

Some agencies have their own Web site. For example, information about job opportunities for the United States Postal Service is on their Web site at www.usps.com/employment. Application employment forms are accessible for download from this Web site.

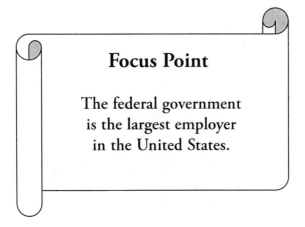

Focus Point

The federal government is the largest employer in the United States.

PART TWO

Becoming Involved

Chapter 3
Seeking Federal Employment

If you are seeking employment with the federal government, it is important to note that all persons employed by the federal government are required to undergo a background investigation. The hiring agency or the Federal Office of Personnel Management (OPM) will look into your present lifestyle and your past activities. The federal government is an Equal Opportunity Employer and prohibits discrimination in hiring practices, as well as in the workplace environment.

The job for which you are applying will dictate the scope of the investigation. If you apply for an entry-level position, there will be a less extensive examination of your background. For example, a clerical position involving no access to confidential information dictates a less intensive inspection of your background. On the other hand, a position that requires national security access, or public contact such as law enforcement, requires a greater scrutiny of your background.

Citizenship Requirements

Applications for federal employment may not be accepted from non-citizens. Title 5 of the U.S. Code, General Provisions:

(a) No person shall be admitted to the competitive examination unless such person is a citizen or national of the United States.
(b) No person shall be given any appointment in the competitive service unless such person is a citizen or national of the United States.
(c) OPM may, as an exception to this rule and to the extent permitted by law, authorize the appointment of aliens to positions in the competitive service when necessary to promote the efficiency of the service in specific cases or for temporary appointments.

Agencies considering non-citizens for federal positions must meet the requirements of immigration law, the Appropriations Act ban on paying certain non-citizens, and the executive order restriction on appointing non-citizens in the competitive service.

For initial investigations, it is the responsibility of the hiring agency to corroborate the applicant's date and place of birth by viewing a birth certificate and/or checking other government statistical records.

The Initial Application Process

When applying for a specific job, the applicant is required to submit a resume or complete Optional Application for Federal Employment Form OF612. Information on what must be contained in the resume or OF612 is available for download on the OPM Web site, under "Job Search." The information required for all applications for federal employment includes:

- Job Vacancy Specifics
- Personal Information
- Work Experience
- Education
- Other Education Completed
- Other Qualifications
- Any Other Information Specified in the Vacancy Announcement

It is important to note that government laws and procedures are ever changing. What is applicable today may not apply tomorrow. If you have questions about current laws or the process of a particular agency, be sure to check directly with that agency.

Focus Point

To apply for a federal job, you must submit a resume or complete federal form OF612.

Chapter 4
The Application Process

Persons employed by the federal government are required to be reliable, trustworthy, and of good conduct and character. They must also be loyal to the United States government. One should remember that federal employment is a privilege, and not a right.

Once a person meets employment eligibility requirements and is offered a position, agencies and departments have a duty to request a background or personnel security investigation. The size and scope of the investigation depends upon the request of the agency's security officer. It also depends on the job position. As stated in chapter 3, the more access an employee will have to confidential government information, the more in depth the background investigation will be.

Fingerprint Requirements

The law requires that all federal employees have their fingerprints taken. Either the Federal Office of Personnel Management or the hiring agency accepts this responsibility. In some cases, you may go to a police agency to be fingerprinted. Agencies send the prints to the Federal Bureau of Investigation (FBI) to ensure that there is no criminal activity involving the applicant found in their records. There are currently three submission formats for fingerprints:

- Hard Card—an older ink or chemical method
- Card Scan—a scanned image of a hard card
- Live Scan—a newer digital, paperless technology

Security Forms

Before a security background investigation can begin, an applicant is required to complete another form providing further information about his or her personal history. The three personnel security forms most widely used are:

- **Questionnaire for Non-Sensitive Positions**, Standard Form (SF85)
- **Questionnaire for Public Trust Positions**, Standard Form (SF85P)
- **Questionnaire for National Security Positions**, Standard Form (SF86)

Completion of the questionnaire is essential. The background investigation is part of the job requirement. Obviously, if a person does not complete the form, the job opportunity is lost.

It is important to fill out the questionnaire as completely and accurately as possible. Applicants must fill in all dates contained in the form. They must also explain gaps in time. For example, if someone worked at ABC Company from June to December 2003, and his or her next job was at DEF Company from May to September 2004, an agency will want to know what activity occurred from January to May 2004.

Honesty is of the utmost importance. While an unintended omission may not have a large negative impact, a deliberate lie or falsification of information will probably have a detrimental result. In addition, the U.S. Criminal Code (title 18, section 10011) provides that knowingly falsifying or concealing a material fact is a felony, which may result in fines of up to $10,000 and/or five years imprisonment.

Focus Point

It is important to fill out the background questionnaire as completely and accurately as possible.

Chapter 5
Contents of the Standard Forms

The three government forms previously mentioned contain some identical questions. However, questions for more sensitive security positions require further information from the applicant.

Information Sheet

Each of the three standard forms contains an information sheet explaining:

- Purpose of this Form
- Authority to Request this Information
- The Investigative Process
- Instructions for Completing this Form
- Final Determination of Your Eligibility
- Penalties for Inaccurate or False Statements
- Disclosure of Information

The cover sheet for public trust positions and national security positions includes information advising that some investigations will include an applicant interview. More information about the applicant interview is in chapter 10. These forms are available for downloading on the Office of Personnel Management Web site by clicking on "Federal Forms." Following are lists of required information an applicant must provide, depending on which standard form he or she is completing:

Questionnaire for Non-Sensitive Positions
Standard Form 85

1. Full Name

2. Date of Birth

3. Place of Birth

4. Social Security Number

5. Other Names Used (Dates and Times)

6. Sex (Female or Male)

7. Citizenship

8. Where You Have Lived

9. Where You Went To School

10. Your Employment Activities (Five-Year Period)

11. People Who Know You Well (References)

12. Your Selective Service Record (Registration)

13. Your Military History

14. Illegal Drugs (Usage)

Questionnaire for Public Trust Positions
Standard Form 85P

1. Full Name

2. Date of Birth

3. Place of Birth

4. Social Security Number

5. Other Names Used

6. Other Identification Information (Physical Description)

7. Telephone Numbers (Work and Home)

8. Citizenship

9. Where You Have Lived (Back Seven Years)

10. Where You Went To School (Back Seven Years)

11. Your Employment Activities (Back Seven Years)

12. Your Employment Record (Reason for Leaving)

13. People Who Know You Well

14. Your Marital Status (Current and Past Spousal Information)

Standard Form SF85P continued

15. Your Relatives (Name, Date of Birth, Country of Birth, Citizenship, and Address)

16. Your Military History

17. Selective Service Record

18. Your Investigations Record (U.S. Government)

19. Foreign Countries You Have Visited

20. Your Police Record

21. Illegal Drugs (Useage)

22. Your Financial Record (Delinquencies, Liens, Or Judgments)

Questionnaire for National Security Positions
Standard Form 86

1. Full Name

2. Date of Birth

3. Place of Birth

4. Social Security Number

5. Other Names Used

6. Other Identifying Information (Physical Description)

7. Telephone Numbers

8. Citizenship

9. Where You Have Lived

10. Where You Went to School

11. Your Employment Activities (Back 7–10 Years)

12. People Who Know You Well (References)

13. Your Spouse (Current and Former Spousal Information)

14. Your Relatives and Associates (Names, Date of Birth, Country of Birth, Citizenship, and Address)

15. Citizenship of Your Relatives and Associates

Standard Form SF86 continued

16. Your Military History

17. Your Foreign Activities (Business and Financial)

18. Foreign Countries You Have Visited (Reasons)

19. Your Military Record

20. Your Selective Service Record

21. Your Medical Record

22. Your Employment Record (List Reasons for Leaving)

23. Your Police Record

24. Your Use of Illegal Drugs and Drug Activity

25. Your Use of Alcohol

26. Your Investigations Record (U.S. Government)

27. Your Financial Record (Bankruptcies, Liens, and
    Judgments)

28. Your Financial Delinquencies

29. Public Record Civil Court Actions

30. Your Association Record (Loyalty Questions)

Certification

Each of the questionnaires for the above standard forms contains a certification at the end that reads:

Certification That My Answers Are True

My statements on this form, and any attachments to it, are true, complete, and correct to the best of my knowledge and belief and are made in good faith. I understand that a knowing and willful false statement on this form can be punished by fine or imprisonment or both (See section 1001 of title 18, United States Code).

Signature (Sign in ink) _____

Date _____

Waivers and Authorizations

Incorporated in each standard form, there is an authorization that the applicant is required to read carefully, and then sign and date. The title of this form is: **Authorization for Release of Information.**

By signing the release of information form, an applicant authorizes any investigator, special agent, or other duly accredited representative of the authorized federal agency conducting the background investigation to obtain any information relating to his or her activities. This includes obtaining information from individuals, schools, residential management agents, employers, criminal justice agencies, credit bureaus, consumer reporting agencies, collection agencies, retail business establishments, or other sources. In addition, it authorizes investigators, special agents, and federal agencies to request and receive criminal record information. This form also states that sources of information and the information released by records' custodians are for official use by the federal government only for the purpose provided in the standard form that is signed, and that it may be re-disclosed by the government only as authorized by law.

If an applicant fails to sign this authorization, the background investigation cannot proceed. Note that individuals, private companies, and some government agencies are not required to produce information; however, they are usually cooperative.

This general authorization is most often sufficient to complete the investigation. However, if issues arise during the investigation, other specific releases may be required. This might include a specific release for authorization to obtain medical information, information regarding drug or alcohol treatment, tax information, and financial records other than through credit unions.

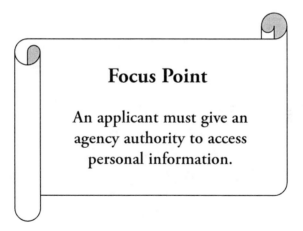

Focus Point

An applicant must give an agency authority to access personal information.

PART THREE

Let the Investigation Begin

Chapter 6
Some Investigative Mandates

The government must adhere to the following federal laws when conducting employment background investigations. The following is a brief description of applicable laws:

Freedom of Information Act (FOIA)

In 1966, Congress passed the Freedom of Information Act. The FOIA, title 5 of the United States Code, section 552, generally provides that any person has the right to request access to federal agency records or information. All agencies of the U.S. government are required to disclose records upon receiving a written request, except those records that are protected by law from disclosure. There are many exemptions to the act. Among the exclusions is the release of classified national security information, trade secrets and other confidential business information, personal information that would violate a person's privacy, and law enforcement investigation information. In addition, the act excludes Congress, the federal court systems, and the president's immediate staff from complying with release of information. This act does not require a federal agency to release background investigations reports to the public.

Privacy Act

In 1974, Congress passed the Privacy Act. The purpose of this law is to protect an individual's right to privacy regarding their personal information on file with federal government agencies. Prior to passage of this act, information provided by persons interviewed during the investigation was deemed confidential. In addition, copies of the investigation report were not given to the applicant. The Privacy Act now provides that an individual may have access to his or her own personal information. Therefore, an applicant who is the subject of a federal background investigation has the right to request and receive a copy of his or her investigation report. Investigators are now required to tell personal contact sources that their interview is conducted pursuant to the Privacy Act. Therefore, the information provided during the interview will be contained in the report furnished to the applicant. Sources can request that information they provide remain confidential. In rare cases, the source is granted confidentiality.

The questionnaires or standard forms contain the following text. "Disclosure of Information: The information you give us is for the purpose of investigating you for a national security position; we will protect it from unauthorized disclosure. The collection, maintenance, and disclosure of background investigative information is governed by the Privacy Act. The agency which requested the investigation and the agency which conducted the investigation have published notices in the Federal Register describing the systems of records in which your records will be maintained. You may obtain copies of the relevant notices from the person who gave you this form. The information on this form, and information we collect during the investigation may be disclosed without your consent as permitted by the Privacy Act (5 USC 552a (b)) and as follows …" The form includes eleven routinely authorized uses for disclosing personal information. Most deal with the release of information to federal, state, or local government agencies for official purposes.

Right to Financial Privacy Act

In 1978, this act became law. It provides that the applicant sign a specific authorization for release of financial information, naming the financial institution and granting permission to the institution to release their personal financial information. This act applies to such institutions as banks, credit unions, savings and loan companies, and other financial institutions. The investigator must provide a copy of the release to the financial institution. A specific authorization is not required to obtain credit bureau or collection agency information.

Congress passed this act, later codified in 12 U.S.C. 3401, in response to a Supreme Court decision that found bank customers had no legal right to privacy for their personal information held by financial institutions. This consumer protection law is largely procedural and requires government agencies to provide notice and an opportunity to object before a bank or other institution can disclose personal financial information to a government agency. In order to obtain access to copies of information contained in a customer's finance records, a government authority generally must first obtain one of the following:

- An authorization signed and dated by the customer that identifies the records, the reason the records are being requested, and the customer's rights under the act
- An administrative subpoena or summons
- A search warrant
- A judicial subpoena
- A formal, written request by a government agency (to be used only if no administrative summons or subpoena authority is available)

Fair Credit Reporting Act (FCRA)

In 1971, Congress passed this act found in federal law 15 U.S.C. 168. This act regulates the collection, dissemination, and use of consumer credit information. The purpose is to protect consumers' privacy and to ensure the accuracy, relevancy, and proper utilization of consumer reports. This act, among other things, allows federal agencies to obtain information from credit bureaus for employment and national security purposes. No release from the applicant is necessary to obtain information in their credit reports. In 1996, Congress amended this act to require further rules that employers must follow in obtaining consumer reports. The FCRA now requires employers to give the consumer a clear and conspicuous written notification that states the employer may obtain a consumer credit report. An applicant also has the right to dispute information contained in the credit report.

Consumer reporting agencies are entities that collect and disseminate information about consumers to be used for credit evaluations and certain other purposes. Under FCRA, they have responsibilities that include:

- Provide information to consumers about information contained in the agency's files and verify any negative information disputed by the consumers.
- If negative information is removed as a result of a consumer dispute, it cannot be reinstated without notification to the consumer.
- Negative information cannot be retained in a consumer's file for an excessive period.

The act also regulates information furnishers. Most often, information furnishers are creditors with whom consumers have some kind of agreement (i.e., mortgage lenders, auto finance companies, etc.). Under FCRA, information furnishers may only report information about a consumer under the following conditions:

- They must provide complete and accurate information to credit agencies.
- They assume the duty to investigate disputed information from the consumer.
- Within thirty days, they must inform consumers about any negative information that has been placed on a consumer credit report.

The Fifth Amendment

This Constitutional amendment gives citizens the right to protect themselves against self-incrimination. Therefore, an applicant cannot be compelled to discuss information obtained during the investigation, whether positive or negative. However, if an applicant chooses not to clarify or explain derogatory information, it might adversely affect their job opportunity. See the Fifth Amendment in its entirety as follows:

Amendment V of the United States Constitution

No person shall be held to answer for a capital, or otherwise infamous crime, unless on a presentment or an indictment of a grand jury, except in cases arising in the land or naval forces, or in the militia, when in active service in time of war or public danger, nor shall any person be subject for the same offense to be twice put in jeopardy of life or limb; nor shall be compelled in any criminal case to be a witness against himself, nor be deprived of life, liberty, or property, without due process of law; nor shall private property be taken for public use without just compensation.

Focus Point

Congress approved government mandates to protect the rights of individuals.

Chapter 7
Behind the Scenes

The goal of the federal government is to conduct a background investigation that provides comprehensive coverage of a person's employment suitability, character, trustworthiness, and loyalty for government agencies and departments.

The First Steps

When a federal agency receives a completed questionnaire or standard form, their job is to determine the type and scope of an applicant's background investigation. The agency's security officer usually assumes this responsibility. Many positions require a security clearance to access government information. A security clearance allows access to classified government information as the person has a need to know in order to perform his or her official duties.

Types of Security Clearances

- **Confidential (C)**: Access to information, which if improperly disclosed could cause minor damage to national security. This is the basic clearance level.
- **Secret (S)**: Access to information, which if improperly disclosed could cause serious damage to national security.
- **Top Secret (TS)**: Access to information, which if improperly disclosed could cause irreparable damage to national security.
- **Q or L Clearances**: Primarily grants access to nuclear programs and information of the Department of Energy.

After the agency determines the type of investigation needed, it submits a request for a background or personnel security investigation. Some agencies choose to do their own investigations; however, most agencies delegate the authority to the United States Office of Personnel Management (OPM).

Investigation Categories and Coverage Period

Again, access to classified or confidential information is the name of the game. The level of access determines which investigation category is assigned. It also dictates the years and length of the coverage period.

Each type of investigation has a Basic Coverage Period that specifies how much of the applicant's past is examined (depending on the job applied for). Some types of investigations also have a Personal Coverage Period that refers to the number of years of activity to cover by personal contact or interview. The investigator must also review and report written records of activity within both coverage periods.

Following is a list of some investigation categories and coverage periods:

- **Limited Background Investigation (LBI):** This type of investigation is primarily for Moderate Risk Public Trust and Non-Critical Sensitive positions. Both the Basic Coverage Period and the Personal Coverage Period are three years.
- **Minimum Background Investigation (MBI):** This type of investigation is primarily for Moderate Risk Public Trust or Non-Critical Sensitive positions. The Basic Coverage Period is five years. The Personal Coverage requires only an applicant interview.
- **Background Investigation (BI):** This type of investigation is primarily for High Risk Public Trust positions. Both the Basic Coverage Period and the Personal Coverage Period are five years.
- **Single Scope Background Investigation (SSBI):** This category of investigation is to meet investigation requirements for positions requiring access to Top Secret and Sensitive Compartmented Information. The Basic Coverage Period is ten years. The Personal Coverage Period is seven years.

Just who organizes and tracks investigations? See the next chapter to find out.

Focus Point

The size and scope of the investigation depends upon access to confidential government information.

Chapter 8

The Federal Investigations Processing Center (FIPC)

A federal agency forwards the request for investigation, as well as the applicant's completed questionnaire or standard form to the Federal Office of Personnel Management's Federal Investigators Processing Center (FIPC). FIPC plays a major role in the investigation process. FIPC enters information from the completed questionnaire into their mainframe computer system known as the Personnel Investigation Processing System (PIPS). FIPC assigns an item number to each piece of information that requires verification and/or further information. The generated report is referred to as the case papers. As the investigation proceeds, FIPC enters new data and the Case Assignment Tracking Screen (CATS) automatically displays updated information on each case.

FIPC completes many investigation items requiring adjudication. FIPC begins their part of the investigation by completing National Agency Checks (NAC) on the applicant, often referred to as the "subject." The scope of the NAC varies, depending on the type of investigation. This is to check whether there is any detrimental information on file with federal agencies or financial institutions. Following are typical examples of national agencies checks and financial records searches that FIPC conducts in order to meet federal investigation requirements:

- Defense Clearance and Investigations Index (DCII)
- Federal Bureau of Investigation Index (FBII)
- Federal Bureau of Investigation Fingerprint Index (FBIF)
- Security/Suitability Investigations Index (SII)
- Verification of Citizenship with the State Department, Immigration, and Naturalization Service (INS), and/or other records as appropriate
- Credit Bureau record searches

Inquiries by Letter

For positions that have limited access to confidential information, such as the Limited Background category, FIPC sends inquiry letters to employers, property owners, law enforcement agencies, educational institutions, and references to verify information listed in the applicant's Standard Form. The letters also request comments regarding the applicant's character and performance. If any negative information is found in the above agencies checks, or in the inquiry letters of return, FIPC assigns the items to a field office for further investigation.

Field Assignments

The Federal Office of Personnel Management (OPM) has some in-house personnel to do their fieldwork. However, the Federal Acquisition Regulation gives them contract authority to have private investigation firms assist them. OPM's Federal Investigations Services Division often assigns a great deal of field investigation work to one of their contract investigation firms.

As stated earlier, the most prominent and widely used contract firm is United States Investigations Services, Inc. (USIS), headquartered in Falls Church, Virginia. OPM provides training and issues investigators proper identification.

For investigation categories that require in-depth investigations and fieldwork, FIPC assigns many items that require coverage to various field offices throughout the United States. These categories include Minimum Background Investigations, Background Investigations, and Single Scope Background Investigations. FIPC also assigns other work requested by federal agencies to field offices.

Focus Point

OPM oversees most agency investigations. FIPC organizes, assigns, and tracks case data.

Chapter 9
Obtaining Record Information

Viewing and reporting information found in records is one of the most effective ways of scrutinizing an applicant's background. The previous chapter explained FIPC's role in obtaining record information. Combine that with the investigator's role during the field investigation and you have a pretty well-rounded picture of the applicant's past.

Common Record Sources

- Court Records
- Department of Motor Vehicle Records
- Educational Records including transcripts
- Employment Records
- Law Enforcement Records
- Military Records
- Professional Licenses Records (state or local)

Government policies and laws are continually changing. The employment background investigation process requires compliance with the law. Chapter 6 explained some federal mandates that must be adhered to. State and local laws vary according to the government policies of each state or local jurisdiction. Below is a brief overview of some general requirements for obtaining state or local records.

Public Records

Accessing public records is the least restrictive way of obtaining information. Public records include information contained in court records, both criminal and civil. Usually, local, state, and federal court records can be viewed, and copies obtained, without presenting an applicant's written authorization giving permission to review his or her records. Public records include information regarding criminal filings, civil lawsuits, divorce filings, bankruptcy liens and judgments.

The process of obtaining juvenile court criminal records differs. Some states require a court order prior to allowing access to juvenile records. Other states require a release from the applicant authorizing an investigator to review his or her record. Most states define a juvenile as someone under the age of eighteen.

Law Enforcement Records

State laws and local ordinances differ on the process of releasing adult law enforcement records. Many jurisdictions require written permission from the applicant before providing arrest or incident reports. Some government agencies only release arrest record information after a conviction in a court of law. Many law enforcement agencies allow release of arrest information without a court conviction when an applicant is applying for a law enforcement or national security position. Obtaining juvenile arrest records from a law enforcement agency is more complex. However, if investigators follow agency procedures, records are often accessible.

Private Industry Records

While many laws control the release of information found in government records, there are few restrictions upon private industry. Some companies or corporations are willing to allow investigators to view employment records; however, many require a written release or waiver from the applicant. This is to protect employers from becoming involved in a lawsuit. Some companies permit personal interviews with supervisors, and in some cases co-workers. Some corporation and company policies only allow verification of employment by releasing the employee's date of employment and termination of employment.

It is important to note that while an investigator may not have access to records, positive or negative information is discovered during personal interviews.

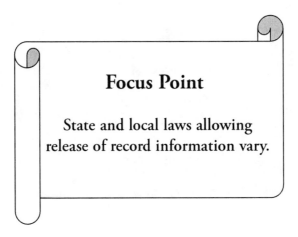

Focus Point

State and local laws allowing release of record information vary.

PART FOUR

Investigators at Work

Chapter 10
The Field Investigation

Once the appropriate field offices receive their case assignments and request to investigate various items, the field investigation begins. The field office assigns items requiring work within their jurisdiction to investigators using their assigned staff identification numbers. The work is assigned using secured government computers. As you can see, portions of an investigation may take place in various parts of the country, with many investigators covering the applicant's activities.

The Personal Applicant Interview

Most investigation categories require an interview of the applicant. An investigator assigned from the regional field office where the applicant resides or works calls the applicant to schedule an interview. The purpose of the interview is to verify all information in the questionnaire, fill in any time gaps, and resolve any questions or issues. The investigator will ask the applicant to bring some personal information to the interview, such as photo identification showing the applicant's name, date of birth, and current address.

A driver's license is acceptable. The investigator might also ask the applicant to bring names and telephone numbers of people not listed as references on the questionnaire. The investigator may also include a request for copies of information relating to diplomas or other public record information.

At the start of the interview, the investigator is required to show the applicant his or her credentials for identification purposes. Next, the investigator verifies the applicant's identification. The investigator then administers an oath and asks the applicant to attest or affirm that the information he or she is about to give is true, correct, and complete. This authority is found in the United States Code, title 5, section 1306. If the applicant refuses to take an oath, the investigator may administer an unsworn declaration asking the applicant to certify, under penalty of perjury, that the information he/she is about to provide will be true and complete. The unsworn declaration is authorized in United States Code, title 28, section 1746. The applicant should be honest because during the investigation, discrepancies or untruths will be uncovered through record checks and/or personal interviews.

Activity Coverage

All types of background investigations require standard measures of the applicant's past activity. The purpose is to develop a well-rounded picture of the applicant. It is important to determine the applicant's character and reputation, honesty and trustworthiness, conduct and behavior, judgment and reliability, mental and emotional stability, and financial responsibility. It is necessary to know that the applicant is a law-abiding citizen and does not have a problem with drug or alcohol abuse.

Following are items that require scrutiny and are reported for all types of investigations:

Law Enforcement: These record checks are usually the first item investigators will complete. The purpose is to determine if there were any incident reports or arrests within an agency's jurisdiction. This requires record searches with law enforcement agencies of the applicant's main activities, including employment, education, and residences. Investigators are required to give a copy of the Authorization for Release of Information to each agency. If any reports or negative information is uncovered, there is a follow-up to obtain the court records. Further investigation may also include conducting interviews with those involved in the incident. All record information, including juvenile information and that outside the coverage period, must be reported.

Court Records: These searches include checking for financial delinquencies, divorce, or other criminal and civil filings. Investigators obtain copies of the records and include the information in their investigation report.

Employment: Information relating to employment must be reported and verified for the required coverage periods. Investigators will contact employers and schedule interviews with supervisors and co-workers. The investigator is required to give the employer a copy of the Authorization for Release of Information. The investigator reviews employment records, if the employer gives permission. Most employers are cooperative in providing these records. Investigators also review and report employment evaluations and any other pertinent positive or negative information in the file. Once you are offered a position, and before the background investigation, it is recommended that you tell your employee that you are seeking federal employment and that a background investigation will take place. The employer will more likely be cooperative when contacted. A few companies have standard policies of providing limited information, such as only disclosing date of hire and date of termination of employment. In such cases, the investigator will try to find information through contact with co-workers. Verification of self-employment is required in the same manner as employment.

Investigators check for a business license or necessary credentials, and schedule interviews with people who know the applicant's business activities.

Education: If this is the main activity of the applicant, investigators interview instructors and fellow classmates. Investigators frequently review campus police records to determine if there were ever any problems on campus. Investigators also review attendance records and obtain grade transcripts. It is necessary to provide an Authorization for Release of Information to the educational institutions. If education is not the applicant's main activity, investigators need only report and verify educational records.

Residence: Verification is required and accomplished by interviewing neighbors at the present residence, and sometimes other neighbors where the applicant lived within the time required by the type of investigation. Some investigation categories require a one-year period, others three or five. When applicable, the investigator views and obtains records. For example, if the applicant resides in an apartment, the investigator will review and report information in rental records to verify dates of residence and rental payment records. Investigators look for and report complaints and any positive or negative information. When possible, investigators interview the apartment manager. The signed Authorization for Release of Information is given to the property owner or person in charge of the records.

References: The investigator interviews persons listed in the applicant's questionnaire as "People Who Know You Well." The investigator will locate and interview other persons not listed in the case papers, but who have extensive or regular contact with the applicant. These interviews provide a comprehensive overview of the applicant's behavior and activities (including employment, education, and residences). This also includes obtaining information about unstructured activities such as sport participation, etc. Investigators must do follow-up work to confirm or deny, and report any discrepancies or derogatory allegations.

Additional Activity Coverage for Public Trust Positions (SF85P) and National Security Positions (SF86)

Additional information is required to ensure there are no issues that might influence an applicant to act against national security interests.

Selective Service Records: Investigators check records to ensure that applicants comply with the Selective Service Military Act registration requirement that men born in 1960 and later, and who have reached their eighteenth birthday, must register. If there is knowing or willful non-compliance, the applicant is not eligible for appointment to a position in an executive agency. The applicant may present a written explanation disputing that his failure to register was knowing or willful. The final determination lies with the Federal Office of Personnel Management (OPM).

Military History Records: Investigators verify dates and types of service, rank and other activity. This is accomplished by viewing the applicant's form DD214, the standard separation document of the United States Military. The full name of the document is Defense Department Form 214. The form contains a complete record of time served in the military. For example:

- Date and place of entry into active duty
- Date and place of release from active duty
- Last duty assignment and rank
- Military job specialty
- Military education
- Medals, awards, decorations, etc.
- Separation information such as type of separation or discharge, and reinstatement eligibility

Any negative information or discrepancies require further investigation.

Former Spouses: Investigators interview former spouses of the applicant if he or she was divorced within the last ten years. This is to determine the reason for the divorce and to see if there were, or are, any problems such as abuse or non-support. Investigators also inquire as to the applicant's reliability, trustworthiness, and loyalty to the U.S. government.

Foreign Association: During the personal applicant interview and source interviews, the investigator asks questions to determine if the applicant has in the past, or now has any affiliation with persons or organizations dedicated to the violent overthrow of the United States government. Positive or negative affiliation information is often revealed during the applicant interview or from inquiries during personal contact interviews.

Loyalty: During the Personal Subject Interview, the investigator discusses the applicant's dedication to the United States. During personal interviews, the investigator queries if there is anything in the applicant's background that might subject him or her susceptible to coercion or blackmail. It is important to determine that there is no reason to question the applicant's loyalty to the United States. United States Code, title 5, section 7311 states: An individual may not accept or hold a position in the government of the United States or the government of the District of Columbia if he:

(1) advocates the overthrow of our constitutional form of government;
(2) is a member of an organization that he knows advocates the overthrow of our constitutional form of government;

(3) participates in a strike or asserts the right to strike, against the government of the United States or the District of Columbia; or

(4) is a member of an organization of employees of the government of the United States or of individuals employed by the government of the District of Columbia that he knows asserts the right to strike against the government of the United States or the government of the District of Columbia.

Focus Point

In order to have a total view of the applicant's background, field investigations take place throughout the United States.

Chapter 11
Additional Agency Requests

Federal agencies may request extra investigative coverage when additional information is needed to help the agency determine a person's qualifications for a certain position. This includes asking specific suitability questions pertaining to a position during all personal interviews. Some examples of these positions and queries to determine an applicant's ability to perform a specific job include:

- **Supervisory positions:** Does the applicant have the ability to communicate effectively, both orally and in writing? Does he/she have the experience and the ability to manage others? Does the person use good judgment and discretion when dealing with others?

- **Law Enforcement positions:** Does he/she have the ability to operate under stress and handle emergencies? Is the applicant mentally stable and physically able to perform the required duties of a police officer? Would the applicant be discreet and professional when dealing with the public? Does he or she use good judgment? Would the applicant have the ability to work independently?

- **Public Trust positions:** Does the applicant have the proper appearance and demeanor to project a good public image? Does he/she possess the ability to communicate effectively orally and in writing? Does the applicant use diplomacy, tact, and good judgment? Is the applicant loyal to the United States government? Would he/she represent the United States favorably?

The above are just a few examples of additional agency requests to determine a person's suitability to perform satisfactorily in a particular job category. Others might include service in a foreign country, investigator positions, undercover operatives, Department of Energy (DOE) positions, and other employment categories.

A Word about Polygraph Examinations

Polygraph screening, commonly referred to as a lie detector test, is used by defense and intelligence agencies. The word polygraph literally means "many writings." Defense and intelligence agencies use this examination to screen applicants who have access to intelligence and security information. Law enforcement agencies use the polygraph examination to determine the honesty of current and future law-enforcement personnel. It is the responsibility of the federal hiring agency to administer the screening using certified polygraph examiners. This is not part of the Officer of Personnel (OPM) background investigation process. Direct any questions regarding the screening process to the federal hiring agency.

Further information about polygraph examinations is on the Web site of the American Polygraph Association at www. polygraph.com.

Focus Point

Agencies may request further items of investigation to determine a person's qualifications for certain positions.

Chapter 12
Uncovering Derogatory Information

Investigators are required to investigate all derogatory information found in records or during interviews. Investigators must also include all derogatory and discrepant information in the report of investigation. This is referred to as "Issue Resolutions." The purpose is to obtain and report reliable facts about the nature, extent, and period of the applicant's involvement in the act. For example, during an interview, a person says that the applicant physically abuses his or her mate. The best way for the investigator to pursue the allegation is to find a police or court record and report the information. In addition, the issues are pursued through the corroboration or denial by the personal testimony of other sources.

Some Statutory Bars to Appointment

Several issues require automatic debarment from federal employment. Most deal with breaches of loyalty and security. Some are for an indefinite time, and some issues have a debarment time—usually three or five years. Some debarment issues include:

- Committing treason against the United States
- Concealment, removal, mutilation, or destruction of public records
- Current excessive or habitual use of alcohol
- Knowing and willful failure of males born after December 31, 1959, to register for military service pursuant to the Selective Service Military Act (see chapter 10)

The above debarment issues and more are found in the United States Code. Several Web sites that include this information are United States Code at www.gpoaccess.gov and U.S. Code Search at uscode.house.gov.

Some Common Derogatory Issues Found During the Background Investigation

The investigator is responsible for pursuing and reporting all derogatory issues found during the investigation. Some of the most common are:

- Criminal and immoral conduct
- Dishonesty
- Disloyalty
- Disruptive and/or violent behavior
- Domestic violence
- Employment misconduct
- Financial irresponsibility
- Habitual use of intoxicants
- Illegal drug use
- Illegal use of firearms/weapons
- Mental and emotional health instability

Sensitive Loyalty and Security Issues

When dealing with a job position that requires access to sensitive or classified information, questions may surface about the applicant's personal life. Such issues include homosexuality, cohabitation, adultery, illegitimate children, etc. These issues, by themselves, are not necessarily suitability issues. However, when there is a possibility that the behavior could affect issues of security, leading to possible susceptibility to coercion or blackmail, the issues are pursued and reported.

Categorizing the Seriousness of Issues

Derogatory issues found during the investigation are categorized by a level of seriousness. The range of seriousness of the classification and the impact it might have on a job opportunity are:

- **Minor**—Not an automatic disqualification
- **Moderate**—Possible disqualification
- **Substantial**—Probable disqualification
- **Major**—Automatic disqualification

Let us explore a derogatory issue regarding the use of intoxicants. An example of a minor issue is a single incident of being drunk in public. A moderate issue is one charge of driving while intoxicated. A substantial issue is the illegal sale of intoxicants. A major issue is a pattern of excessive use of alcohol or drugs. Issue designations are sometimes upgraded when multiple violations are found.

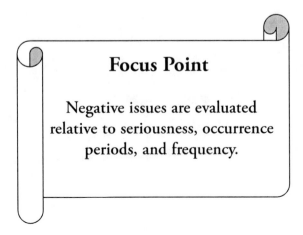

Focus Point

Negative issues are evaluated relative to seriousness, occurrence periods, and frequency.

Chapter 13
Finalizing the Investigation

Many people ask how long an employee background investigation takes. It is difficult to give a precise answer. While federal agencies try to direct investigations in a timely manner by setting deadlines or timeframes for items requiring adjudication, the process may be delayed for various reasons. Sometimes, problems arise when items require further investigation or persons are not available for interviews. I am sure you have heard the expression "Patience is a virtue." This is certainly applicable in this case. However, if more than a few months have passed and you have not received notification of completion, contact the federal agency that requested the investigation. They are usually most helpful in providing information.

The End Is Near

Once all portions of the field investigation are complete, investigators transmit their reports to the Federal Investigations Processing Center (FIPC) via their assigned secure computer.

FIPC reviews the reports for accuracy and ensures that all items are complete. FIPC assembles the Report of Investigation, and sends it to the security office responsible for receiving completed investigation reports.

It is important to remember that the final determination of your suitability is the responsibility of the federal agency that requested the investigation. The questionnaires explain, under Final Determination on Your Eligibility, that "You may be provided the opportunity personally to explain, refute, or clarify any information before a final decision is made." If you wish to refute or clarify any information found in the Report of Investigation, or appeal a decision to deny employment, contact the federal agency. They will explain the procedures you are to follow. On the positive side, when your background investigation is satisfactorily completed, you are eligible for hire with a federal agency. **Congratulations.**

Focus Point

The final suitability determination rests with the federal agency that requested the investigation.

It Is Your Future

Federal career opportunities are abundant. In order to have doors open to you, it is important that you have a clear record, good grades, and a good rapport with neighbors, co-workers, and other acquaintances.

Tips To Prepare For Your Background Investigation

Once you are offered a federal job and are told you are going to have a background investigation, it is a good idea to be prepared. Consider taking the following steps:

- Check your credit report status with a credit-reporting agency to make sure the information in the report is accurate. If there are any discrepancies, make an effort to have them corrected. The U.S. government mandated by law that a consumer is entitled to receive one free credit report every twelve months from each of the nationwide credit-reporting agencies. The three main companies are Equifax, Expedia, and TransUnion. For more information, visit www.annualcreditreport.com.

- Verify that information in your educational transcripts is accurate.

- If employed, inform your employer that you are seeking federal employment. Tell your supervisor that an investigator will ask them to provide information about your conduct and job performance.

- Let your neighbors know that you are applying for a job with the federal government. Advise them that someone may ask them to participate in an interview.

- Tell the people you listed as references that an investigator might interview them to gather information regarding your demeanor and activities.

- If arrested or detained by a law enforcement agency, review the record and ask what you can do to minimize any negative impact. If there is a conviction on your record, check with the court to find out what, if any, action you can take. Some states allow the defendant to apply to have the record expunged. The conviction may remain on court records; however, the fact that you applied to have the record expunged will have a positive effect.

You are in high school or college, a place to study and have fun. However, it is important to consider your future when making choices. In other words, think before you act.

Abbreviations

AA&E	Arms, Ammunition and Explosives Program
CATS	Case Assignment Tracking Screen
CIP	Critical Infrastructure Program
CSC	Civil Service Commission
DCIS	Defense Clearance and Investigations Index
DIS	Defense Investigations Services
DOD	Department of Defense
DOE	Department of Energy
DSS	Defense Security Services
FBI	Federal Bureau of Investigations
FBIP	Federal Bureau of Investigations Fingerprint Index
FBIN	Federal Bureau of Investigations Index
FCRA	Fair Credit Reporting Act
FIPC	Federal Investigations Processing Center
FOIA	Freedom of Information Act
INS	Immigration and Naturalization Services
NAC	National Agency Check
NISP	National Industrial Security Program
PIPS	Personnel Investigation Processing System
SCI	Sensitive Compartmented Information

SII   Security/Suitability Investigation Index

USIS   United States Investigations Services, Inc.

USOPM   United States Office of Personnel Management

USC   United States Code

USPS   United States Postal Services

Index

A

B

D

E

F

H

human resource agency, *See* United States Office of Personnel
Management (OPM)

I

identification, 57, 58

immigration law, 18

imprisonment, 23; *See also* Criminal activity

interviews, 26, 53, 57–58

    of foreign associations, 62

    with former spouses, 62

    and honesty, 58

    for job suitability, 65–66

    of loyalty to U.S., 62–63

    with references, 60

investigations; *See also* background information; interviews; records;
    Standard forms

    categories, 44, 45

    coverage periods, 44, 45

    of derogatory information, 69

    of discrepant information, 69

    field assignments, 48, 57

M

misconduct, 5

N

National Agency Checks (NACS), 47, 48

National Industrial Security Program (NISP), 8

National Intelligence Community Department, 8

National Security, 6

    information, 7

    positions, 22, 26, 30–31, 61

National Security Directive 63, 7

Non-citizens, 18

non-sensitive positions, 22, 27, 45

O

OPM, *See* United States Office of Personnel Management (OPM)

P

personal information, access to, 33

Personnel Investigation Processing System (PIPS), 47

polygraph exams, 66–67

postmaster positions, 6

Privacy Act, 38–39

private industry records, 53

private investigation firms, 8

public records, 52, 70

public service, 5

public trust positions, 22, 26, 28–29, 61, 66

R

records

    court, 59

    educational, 60

    employment, 53

    employment history, 53, 59

    law enforcement, 52–53, 58–59

    military history, 61

    public, 52

    selective service, 61

    sources, 51

resume submission, 18, 19

Right to Financial Privacy Act, 39

S

T

Printed in the United States
131482LV00001B/409-417/P